AF486530

Manners Do Matter

A Guide for Children, Parents, and Politicians

By Linda Waller Holden

Illustrator Michael Riley

ISBN 979-8-88644-822-1 (Paperback)
ISBN 979-8-88644-823-8 (Digital)

Copyright © 2023 Linda Waller Holden
All rights reserved
First Edition

All rights reserved. No part of this publication may be reproduced, distributed, or transmitted in any form or by any means, including photocopying, recording, or other electronic or mechanical methods without the prior written permission of the publisher. For permission requests, solicit the publisher via the address below.

Covenant Books
11661 Hwy 707
Murrells Inlet, SC 29576
www.covenantbooks.com

I dedicate my first book to my husband Blair, who has always encouraged my every endeavor. It is also dedicated to my children, Christopher and Heather, and their children, Ellie, Liv, and Gavin. We have had a lot of laughs and tears about manners over the years! May the laughs continue, and yes, MANNERS DO MATTER.

Love,
Mom

Contents

Introduction

Wouldn't it be nice to live in a world of trust, honesty, and cooperation? A place where people thought before they spoke. A place where we actually listened to each other and tried to understand.

We can. It starts with manners.

As I mature, I see and hear many things I did not see or hear in my youth.

It is important to me to pass on a manner guide to my children, my grandchildren, and the world.

Manners are free, and manners are a way to show kindness and respect. They are not something you just put on and take off like a coat. They should be practiced…daily. They should be a part of YOU every day in every situation.

I hope this book will be helpful to all who read it.

Do I practice everything I have written all of the time? I try and I may fail so I keep on trying.

Etiquette

Don't you just love a BIG word? And a French word at that!
The dictionary says *etiquette* is a code for polite behavior in society.
A good friend of mine says, "Etiquette is your TICKET!"*
This book explains your ticket to being a kind, graceful, polite, courteous, polished, well-behaved, and successful individual.

Speaking of French, do you know what RSVP stands for?
When you receive an invitation to an event, you may see RSVP some place on the invitation.
This means *respondez, s'il vous plait.*

In English, this simply means respond please. It is important to respond yes or no. This will simply help the host or hostess know how many chairs to have, or how many pizzas to order.
At times, you will see RSVP Regrets Only, which means you only need to tell your host if you cannot make the event.

---

* Mrs Geri Sheffey Piedmont Cotillions, Greensboro, NC

Important Words to Know

Kindness

What exactly is kindness, you may ask?
Being kind is caring, acting friendly, being positive, thinking of others, being cordial, compassionate, considerate, and courteous.
How would you describe kindness?
How would you show kindness?

Respect

How is respect demonstrated?
When people are respectful, they are polite. They show appreciation and admiration. Respectful people listen and do not interrupt.
Who do you respect and why?
Who respects you?
How do you know they respect you?

Confidence

How can a person demonstrate confidence?
A confident person stands tall, looks people in the eye, is sure of him or herself, listens and speaks with self-assurance.
When have you felt confident?

Honesty

When we are honest, we tell the truth in spite of the consequences. This is difficult until you practice it enough. Just think before you speak and be brave. Not telling the truth can harm a reputation.

Trustworthy

Trusting people is believing they are honest and relying on them to be supportive in all situations.

Loyalty

Being loyal is being faithful and doing what you say you will do for others, no matter what the consequences. It is standing up for them as a true friend.

Very Important Words

Please and *thank you* are the *most important* words in the English language. You can never say either of these words too much.

I'm sorry are the *most difficult* two words to say in the English language. Saying this demonstrates great self-assurance and kindness.

"Excuse me" is a *must* to say if anyone is interrupting a conversation, or if anyone is accidentally harmed in any way.

Please

Thank you

Greetings

First things first, what do you do when you see someone you want to meet or talk to or when someone comes up to talk to you?

1. *Smile* sincerely. Smile with your eyes as well as your mouth. You can practice in front of a mirror.

2. Gather your courage and say "hello" or "good morning" or "I like your hair or your shirt."

3. Be kind and sincere.
    Be sure to look the person in the eyes with sincerity.
    What if someone does not respond to your greeting? *It is okay.* You did the polite, right thing.
    You were kind and caring. Their reaction is *their* problem. Hopefully they will learn better manners!

4. Be sure to say goodbye, farewell, and see you soon (with a smile).

Practice this today with a family
member or a friend or both!

The Handshake

The handshake is said to have originated in ancient Greece. It was a sign that neither person was carrying a weapon and would cause no harm to the other person. It is also said to be a way of "passing the peace."

In the past, a lot of people shook hands. Lately because of germs and diseases we have become less of a handshaking society.

An elbow or fist bump has become the greeting of choice. I am personally hoping the handshake will return. You can tell a lot about a person by their handshake.

The handshake is important. If someone extends their *right* hand, it is expected that the other person will also extend their *right* hand. This is a symbol of peace, kindness, and respect.

A handshake is solid and firm. Grip the hand sincerely *and* look the other person in the eye *and* don't try to break their hand!

Handshakes display self-confidence and kindness.

Introducing Someone

After or along with the handshake comes the introduction.
A proper polite introduction could go like this:
"Hello, I am Mr. Smith. How are you?"
It is always very nice to add something else. For instance, maybe a comment about the weather or a mutual friend.
Try introducing someone and shaking hands today.

Name tags

As you shake hands and are talking, be sure to maintain eye contact and give a smile. If you happen to have name tags, the correct placement of the name tag is on the *right* shoulder/chest area. When you extend the right hand for a handshake your eyes follow that arm straight to the name tag.

Sitting Politely

Good posture is healthy!
Look at the people sitting or standing around you. Here is the checklist:

- Standing or sitting straight and tall
- Shoulders back
- Head up

Females

- Legs crossed at the ankle
- Knees together as close as possible

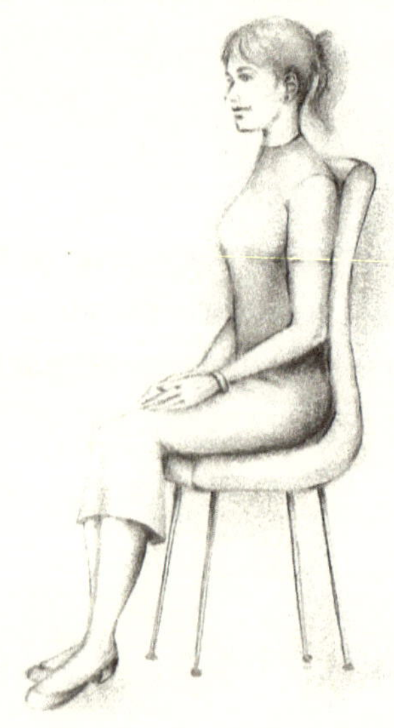

- Feet flat on the floor

Sport coats and suits

If a male is sitting, his jacket can be unbuttoned. This is more comfortable, and the jacket will not wrinkle as quickly.

When a male is standing, he should button the middle button of his jacket. A buttoned jacket shows neatness. It is not flapping in the wind. Men appear more put together, less sloppy, and in shape when their jackets are buttoned.

Politicians often forget to button their jackets when standing. It is a simple rule, and it is maddening when important people do not practice this simple rule.

Easy peasy.

Standing, buttoned.

Sitting, unbuttoned.

This is tricky, time consuming, but very important.

Conversations

Talking with people is so much fun! However, it is just as important to listen.

According to the Webster's Dictionary definition, a conversation is a talk between two or more people in which news and ideas are exchanged.

Listening is difficult to accomplish but a very important part of relationships. It shows respect. (Refer to "Important Words to Know.")

Face-to-face conversations involve eye contact. This is not staring at someone. It is looking at the person, not the surroundings or moving around, but paying attention. This is "active listening." "Passive listening" is just the opposite. It is *not* paying attention, moving around, watching TV, looking at your phone, or acting in a disrespectful manner.

Types of Conversations

Isn't it interesting how our conversations change with our situations, the groups of people we are talking to and the environment surrounding our conversations?
It is important to think about who we are talking to and what we are saying. Conversation involves thinking before we speak.

Casual conversations vs. formal conversations
Friends your age vs. new acquaintances
Family vs. older adults
Sporting events vs. meetings
Home vs. church
Restaurants
Small talk

Socializing is fun, interesting, and essential!
Show interest in each other.
Find out a friend's likes and dislikes. Find out about their family, their pets, places they like to go, things they like to do, or favorite foods.

Phone manners

This one might hurt!
Phones should not be at the dinner table, at home or at a restaurant. They really should not. Dinner is a time for conversation and attention to each other.
I get it. Games are part of keeping children and adults happy. I promise, for several generations, children learned to be happy or at least fake it and be part of the family without a phone at the table. (I will give a pass to a phone on vibrate in a pocket and only responded to in an emergency.)
As far as phone conversations, they should be answered cordially with kindness, acceptance, and respect.
Remember the most important words: *please* and *thank you*!

Conversations Without Words

There is more to conversations than words! Think about it for a minute.

Body language

Body language is defined as the process of communicating nonverbally through conscious or unconscious gestures and movements. People can be perceived as aggressive or non-aggressive and assertive or non-assertive depending on body language. Pay attention to facial and body movements. Watch out for pointing, fists, leaning on something, crossed arms, pacing, or shuffling.
Eyebrow raising, eye contact (or not), mouth twitching, or hair twirling are among habits that can also give clues to what a person is trying to say.
Confidence is portrayed when you are able to look people in the eye and continue to look at them as you talk and as you listen.

Tone

Tone is pitch quality and strength—a modulation of a voice, the attitude or general character of a place or thing.
The tone of a conversation is also important.
Voice level and intonations can send a message, and it might not be the message that is intended. Try this experiment: say "I love you" loudly and with anger in your voice. Now, say the same thing quietly and with a pleasant voice.
Which do you think will be perceived in a positive way?

Texts

Texting is tricky.

First of all, it is *not* private. Do not text anything you would not want made public. It is too easy to save, copy and paste, and send. In a matter of seconds, lives can be ruined and friendships can be lost. No ugly inappropriate words should be used in a text. No mean comments. No photos that you would not share with your grandmother should ever be sent to anyone. Texts are easily misunderstood or misconstrued, so choose your words carefully.

Gossip

Share only positive information about people.
Remember what mothers always say, "If you can't say anything nice, don't say anything at all."
And "if you wouldn't say it to them, don't say it about them."
We all say things at times we are not proud of saying. Here is where the "I am sorry" is very important. Also, daily acts of kindness are a must.

Name Calling

There is no need to use ugly words in a conversation or to say derogatory things about people. Adults need to remember this. Unfortunately, parents, political figures, and people we all look up to and admire need to remember this too and say "I'm sorry" if they are guilty or have hurt someone.

Peer Pressure

So what are peers?

Peers are the people, usually around your age, who you like to be around. They are your friends. Sometimes friends want you to do things or say things or act a certain way. Sometimes the things they want you to do may not be good choices, or they may not feel exactly right.

You might feel pressured into doing these things.

Do not let ANYONE make you do ANYTHING you do not want to do or say.

If YOU choose to do something, that is one thing. That is your decision. If you allow someone else coerce (make) you, that is peer pressure.

Peer pressure can result in the loss of friends, hurt feelings, and confused personal convictions.

It is always okay to say, "No, thank you. That is not what I want to do or say or the way I want to act." Then you can add, "If you are really my friend, you will understand and allow me to be me."

Please stand up for yourself and your beliefs.

Table Manners

The table…one of the most important places for good manners!

Impress

Males should pull out the chair and hold it for any/all females at the table as they sit down.
Females should sit to the right of the male they came with to the table.

Once seated

All people seated at the table should put their napkins in their lap.
If you leave the table, the napkin goes on your chair. At the end of the meal, replace the napkin on the left of the plate.
No elbows on the table…ever.
Chew with your mouth closed. No one wants to see food!
Hold your fork like a pencil, not a shovel. Do not use your fork like a pointer.
Break your bread into a few pieces and butter one small piece at a time.
Remember, do not reach! Use your words, "Please pass the potatoes."
Pass to the right (counterclockwise) if you are passing food at the table.
Use utensils from the outside in. (The salad fork is the small fork next to the dinner fork. The soup spoon is the spoon next to the teaspoon.)

Table Tips

Look at the illustration below!

Now make a *b* with your left hand by touching your index finger to your thumb and extending your other fingers. That *b* can remind you that your bread plate goes on the left of your dinner plate!

Now make a *d* with your right hand. That *d* can remind you that your drink goes on the right of your dinner plate and above your spoon and fork!

This is an easy tip when you are at dinner and cannot remember which is your bread and butter plate, or which is your water glass. Simply put your hands in your lap and make your *b* and *d!*

Share this with your family and friends. They will thank you for the tip!

How to Set Your Dinner Table

1. Dinner Plates
2. Soup Bowl or Salad Plates
3. Forks, Knives and Spoons
4. Water and Wine Glasses
5. Napkins
6, Bread Plates
7. Dessert Forks and Spoons

Soup

Spoon from your body toward the center of the table.
"Out to sea and back to me!"
You have less of a chance of spilling soup on your lap!

One hand

Unless you are cutting meat, one hand should be on your lap at all times.
At the end of the meal, put all silverware diagonally across your plate. (11:00 to 4:00 position). This way the waiter or hostess knows you are finished with your meal.
I like to turn my fork over so the tines (the part of the fork that you put in your mouth) are resting on the plate as I place it in the 11:00 to 4:00 position.

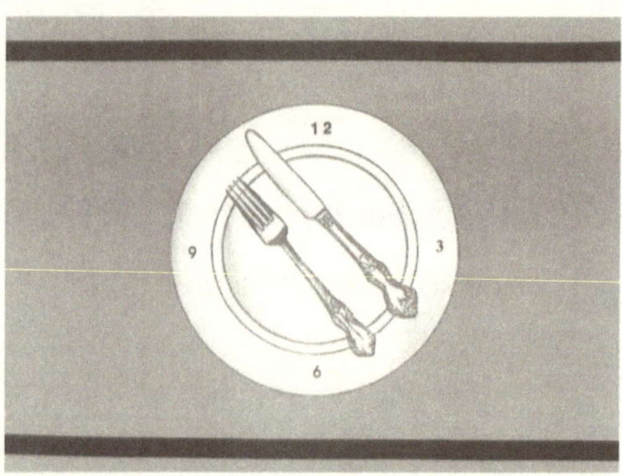

If you need to leave the table for any reason, say, "Excuse me," stand, and place your napkin on your chair.
Now for the fun part.
Every time a female excuses herself from the table, a male should stand, help her with her chair, and button his jacket if he is wearing one. When she returns, he should stand again and help her with her chair.
Guys get lots of exercise!

---

* Mrs. Geri Sheffey Piedmont Cotillions. Greensboro NC

This and That for Here and There

Punctuality

Be on time. In fact, be early!

Sneezing and coughing

Use your "chicken wing" or your elbow!

Doors

Young people should always hold the door for older people at a store, the post office, church, school, and this includes car doors as well! And if you are dating, it is polite and respectful for guys to open the car door for their date.

Dressing

Dress appropriately. PJs are for home, not out and about. Mom and Dad, that means not in the car line at school. Take pride in being clean, neat, and well-groomed.
Dress up to impress when you can and when you want to. Be yourself! Remember you only get one chance to make a first impression.

Standing

Standing up when elderly people enter a room or giving up your seat to an older person on a bus or at a restaurant displays a caring nature and respect.

Compliments

Who else enjoys a nice compliment? If everyone could give (and receive) one compliment every day, I bet self-esteem, confidence, and camaraderie among all of us would skyrocket. Wouldn't it be just as easy to say something nice as to say something derogatory or not say anything at all?

Bathroom

When a person needs to use the bathroom, this is all that needs to be said: "I need to use the bathroom or restroom." Any other description of what the person intends to do in the bathroom is of no importance. No one cares what you need to do in the bathroom.

Thank-you notes

Handwritten notes are the BEST, but an email or thank you text is acceptable. Just a few lines are necessary, but make it somewhat personal.

> Dear Aunt Susie,
>
> Thank you so much for the lovely blue sweater. I am sure I will enjoy wearing it, and I will think of you. I can't wait to see you.
>
> Love,
> Amanda

One More Word About Manners

Are manners important at home? Absolutely.
Manners start at home.
Helping out family members around the house by making your bed, taking out trash, and loading the dishwasher are things that should be expected of all family members. Responsibility has to be taught. Following the rules, being kind, and saying please and thank you are the basics for a happy family and a happy life

Epilogue

Well, I have written all I can think of at this time. I know some of this book may seem old-fashioned and out of date.

I really think it is a shame that we are trying to forget history and manners.

If we all tried to think of others in the same way we think of ourselves and treat others no matter who they are with kindness, I really think the world would be a different place.

It is easy to throw a barb when someone throws one at you. It is difficult to not stoop to their level. It is easy to say ugly things about someone instead of looking for something good or just not saying anything.

I say we all need to be concerned and aware of others around us.

It is easy to not be concerned about the way we eat or look or talk, but is it the right way?

I hope this book will be a help to all who read it.

That is all we can do.

Just remember…MANNERS DO MATTER!

About the Author

Linda Waller Holden loves being around people, but a few years ago she became disillusioned. She did not like seeing the rudeness and the all-about-me-attitude that was prevalent at the time. Her energy, persistence, and creative spirit led her to write a book about something she believes in—the importance of manners. Mrs. Holden hopes people will return to the core values of sharing, caring, being respectful, and having good manners in every situation. Mrs. Holden lives in North Carolina with her husband where she enjoys life and stays as busy as possible, participating in water aerobics, reading, volunteering, and line dancing.

www.ingramcontent.com/pod-product-compliance
Lightning Source LLC
Chambersburg PA
CBHW021814150726
47989CB00004B/1930